Old Heath - Pas

Aerial view of Old Heath Road looking towards Colchester - 2006

Patrick Denney

Old Heath - Past & Present

First published in Great Britain in 2006 by
FRT Publications
13 Abbots Road, Colchester, Essex, CO2 8BE

British Library Cataloguing in Publication Data
A catalogue record for this book is available from the British Library.
ISBN 0-9552944-0-1   ISBN 978-0-9552944-0-2

Front cover illustration - a merging of Old Heath Road - 1931 and 2003
Rear cover illustration - Abbots Road - c.1930

Printed and bound by Print Matrix Ltd
Unit F1, Colchester Business Centre, Colchester, CO4 9HT

Contents

Acknowledgements

A special debt of gratitude is due to Fr Richard Tillbrook of St Barnabas' Church, Old Heath, whose commitment and enthusiasm for the project has been one of the main reasons why the book has finally been brought to publication. His support for the project from day one has been one of unwavering support and encouragement, a commitment which has led to him taking on the role of promoter and publisher.

My thanks is also due to the following individuals for their kind support in providing valued information and photographs for use in the publication:-

Joan Allston, Peter and Sandra Bennett, Graham Broom, Martin and Pauline Broom, Joan Brown, Geoff Crick, Maureen Davey, Pam and Gordon Griggs, Roy and Brenda Keeble, John King, Janet Root, Connie Mercer, Katie Miller, Peter and Maureen Needham, Andrew Phillips, Angela Pilkington, Olwyn Powell, Jan Rayner, Michael and Janet Read, Robin Thomas, Jill Thorogood, Mrs Turrell, John Tyler, Ron and Margaret Wheeler, John Willoughby and Sandra Yeomans.

And finally, a mention for the many anonymous photographers whose works are included in this collection. Without their decision to have captured the moment and to have created a lasting record of the people and landscape of Old Heath, this work would not have been possible.

Patrick Denney
May 2006

Foreword

When the Bishop first offered me the 'Cure of Souls' in the Parish of Old Heath (That's the posh way of saying I was to become the Vicar!) my immediate thought was 'Where on earth is Old Heath?' My only visit to Colchester had been many years ago when I came to a ceremony at the Town Hall on a Sunday, long before shops were allowed to open. So I had little knowledge of Colchester and its people and none at all of the people of Old Heath.

Despite this, the moment I arrived to visit Old Heath, drove around the parish roads and visited the little parish church of St Barnabas, which was described as having no architectural merit on the outside but a warm and beautiful heart inside, I knew that this was where I should be.

Very soon I was welcomed by the people, whether or not they went to church regularly, and I became interested in the history of our village and its people. Amongst the so many friendly members of the community whom I have already met in my three years as your Vicar it has been my good fortune to meet Patrick Denney, our well known local historian.

I shared with him my thoughts that this was an important and interesting community which still, it seemed to me, could claim to be a separate and lively village on the outskirts of, but not swallowed by, Colchester. From that conversation this book was conceived and I hope that you will all enjoy it and learn more about our village of Old Heath, Ancient and original Port of Colchester.

Fr Richard Tillbrook

Historical Background

The area known as Old Heath is situated about two miles from Colchester town centre on the road leading to Rowhedge and Fingringhoe. It covers an area of some 700 acres all lying within the former parish of St Giles, although latterly under the auspices of St Barnabas. In the early 1800s the place was little more than a straggling hamlet surrounded by fields and common land. By the end of the 19th century, however, and with an expanding population, agriculture was in decline and the area was slowly becoming urbanised. Since then it has grown to become what is now a sprawling suburb of Colchester, well populated with a mix of residential housing and light industry.

It is believed that a community, of sorts, has occupied this area since at least Saxon times, although the Domesday reference mentions only the nearby estate of Donyland from which the Old Heath or Battleswick manor is believed to have originated. Also, in numerous documents dating from the 13th century, the area is frequently referred to as the Old Hythe, a name which would appear to derive from the Saxon 'Hetha', signifying a harbour. The historian Morant claimed that the area was so named because "wares and merchandises brought to this town by water used to be unloaded there." Also of interest is the fact that the present Hythe, or former harbour area of the town, was formerly known as the New Hythe, in apparent contrast to an old or earlier port area.

The manorial rights relating to Old Heath were divided between the manors of Battleswick (otherwise Battleshall) and West Donyland, with the boundary separating the two manors following a similar line to the present Old Heath Road. Although the manor of West Donyland was by far the larger of the two, it held less land and enjoyed fewer rights in Old Heath than did Battleswick, the lands of which extended eastward from the main road to the river.

By the onset of the 19th century, Old Heath had still experienced little in the way of commercial growth and remained a relatively obscure district of the town. Even so, it had developed its own identity as a small, but flourishing, agricultural community with a population in 1801 of about 135. The approach to Old Heath from Colchester was by the main Donyland Road (today's Old Heath Road) which led to a gate at the edge of the common. From here an ancient track wound its way across the heath before rejoining the highway at points corresponding to the modern Rowhedge and Fingringhoe Roads. Over the years this large tract of open common land, extending to perhaps 200 acres, had gradually been enclosed until being finally reduced in size to about 75 acres, comprising about one third heath and waste, and the rest marsh. The bulk of the enclosed land was divided between eight farms, ranging in size from about 40-140 acres, the owners of which, in common with various other tenants of the manor, enjoyed certain rights of grazing over the heath and waste land -that is until the land was enclosed by an Act of Parliament in 1811.

Local Industry

Although agriculture remained the predominant commercial activity in Old Heath for much of the 19th century, other industries were gradually becoming established, particularly from the middle years of the century onwards. These included brewing, malting, brick-making and laundry work. However, perhaps the most ambitious undertaking of the entire period was the erection of a malt distillery in 1812 by local businessmen Samuel Bawtree and George Savill.

The building was erected on the site of an old oil mill which straddled the stream separating Old Heath from the neighbouring parish of St Botolph. This oil mill is clearly marked on a map by Chapman and André in 1777 and is known to have been in the possession of the Rootsey family since at least 1732. The new distillery was a great success and was considered to be the largest of its kind in the country. Certainly by the mid 1820s, the historian Thomas Cromwell was able to report that the business was paying an annual tax to the government of at least £100,000 calculated on the amount of wort, or wash, produced at the rate of two shillings per gallon. However, despite these early successes, by about 1840 the business was on the verge of collapse "owing to great losses" and was finally sold off in 1842.

An occupation closely allied to distilling was that of malting and by the mid 19th century the industry had become firmly established in the Hythe and Old Heath areas of the town. One of the largest of these concerns to have developed in Old Heath was that erected in the early 1870s by Richard Cuddon (a brewer from Abberton) on land belonging to the White Hall Estate, which was then in the ownership of the Reverend Holroyd. Part of this original malthouse still survives on the site of Magnets kitchen showroom and warehouse. The present sheltered housing complex standing adjacent to Magnets, and which is known as 'Heathfields House', was erected at the time by Mr Cuddon as his family home.

From around 1850 until the turn of the 20th century the local brick-making industry was also enjoying a period of relative prosperity. Numerous yards were operating along the Colne valley and its tributaries and evidence from local directories show that at least half a dozen sites were being worked at any one time. At Old Heath the industry appears to have peaked during the period 1880-1910, when yards at both New Quay and Cleavelands Farm were providing continuous work for between 10-20 workers. An earlier site has been identified in the area dating back to at least the 1830s, but other than its location, and the fact that it included a purpose made kiln, nothing is known.

The New Quay yard (c.1840-1896) was the earlier of the two sites and can be seen on the 6 inch Ordnance Survey map of 1878. The works extended to about four acres on ground descending toward the river (on the site of the present Haven Road area), with the brickyard buildings arranged in a fairly standard format, i.e. with the kiln being sited downhill of the drying sheds, an arrangement that would have made transferring the heavy barrowloads of bricks to the kiln that much easier.

The Cleavelands Farm site was operating from the late 1880s, and was known as 'Dobson's Brickfield'. *Kelly's Directory for Essex* in 1886 lists George Dobson as both a builder and brick-maker trading from works in Butt Road, Colchester. At what time he acquired the Old Heath site is not known but it must have been before 1891 for in that year 'Dobson's Brickfield' is identified as such on the Old Heath census. Throughout this period the brick-making industry in Old Heath was dominated by the Crick family, all descended from Zachariah Crick who moved into the area in the late 1870s. And at the time of writing some of Zachariah's descendents are still resident in the area.

Yet another industry or trade which flourished locally was laundry work. Originally an activity undertaken almost entirely by women, it was for much of the 19th century the largest single occupational group in Old Heath after agriculture. The earliest evidence relating to the activity is found in the 1851 census when 14 women, more than a third of all working women were described as laundresses. From information received from one elderly Old Heath resident it would appear that many of these women worked at a small laundry located on the Fingringhoe Road, close to the site of the present fish and chip shop. Other women would have worked from their own homes with the laundered items being turned around on a weekly basis. Their customers would have included some of the wealthier families in Colchester and the laundry would have been collected and delivered by handcart (this was often a job for younger members of the family), or otherwise by the Rowhedge carrier who made the journey to town on a daily basis.

One of the main problems facing the laundry workers, however, was being able to obtain an adequate supply of clean water, particularly before the mains were laid on in the village at the turn of the 20th century. The water used would mostly have been collected from local wells or perhaps from the spring-fed water tank (known locally as jumbo) sited on the Old Heath Road near to the current playing field. Larger quantities were collected by horse and cart from Birch Brook at the bottom of 'Jeff's Lane' which ran alongside the water-filled pit on Fingringhoe Road. An interesting comment in this regard can be found in a council report of 1874 when Mr Charles Hawkins, who lived at Maitlands House, spoke regarding the deficiency of water in Old Heath: "My washerwoman, who resides in that place, has to cart every drop of water that she uses more than a mile", he said.

It is not known when the small Fingringhoe Road laundry closed down, but it was probably in the early 1900s, about the same time that brothers George and Herbert Berry began operating a large steam laundry on the site of the old distillery. All the water used for the operation was taken directly from the mill pond and the laundered items were dried in the open air in the adjoining fields. Despite being severely damaged by enemy bombing during the Second World War the laundry continued as a major local employer until its recent closure and demolition to make way for new housing.

Although Old Heath was for many years something of a rural backwater, and isolated from the main town, it didn't suffer from a lack of social amenities. Thanks to the benevolence of local residents such as George Savill, from White Hall, and James Ashwell Tabor, who lived in Old Heath Cottage (where Cottage Drive now stands), the community enjoyed the use of a purpose built schoolhouse from 1837 and from 1869, also a chapel for worship. These were both outreach facilities of Lion Walk Church which had become firmly established in the district before the erection of the new school/chapel building of St Barnabas in 1874.

From around the 1930s, Old Heath rapidly began to lose its rural atmosphere. Until that time the community had been physically separated from the built-up area of the town by a long avenue of elm trees which arched across the road leading up from Cannock Mill. And when one finally emerged from the trees at the Old Heath end it was like being in the open countryside with cows grazing in the fields on either side of the road. In fact, one of the photographs depicted in this collection captures the scene shortly before the last of these trees were removed to make way for housing.

Chapter One
Scenes from the Past

Cannock Hill looking up towards Old Heath in 1993. This is traditionally where the district of Old Heath begins and prior to the 1930s this stretch of road was covered with overhanging elm trees as far up as Whitehall Close, which is just beyond the row of houses on the left.

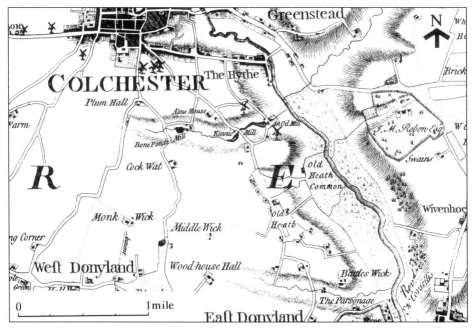

Part of Chapman and Andre's 1777 map of Essex showing the district of Old Heath and Old Heath Common. At this time period the town was still surrounded by hundreds of acres of medieval common and waste land.

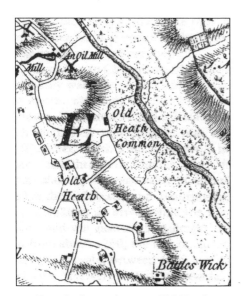

Detail of map showing Old Heath Common and Battleswick Farm. The Oil Mill was adjacent to Distillery Pond.

Battleswick Farm was traditionally the home of the Lord of the Manor.

10

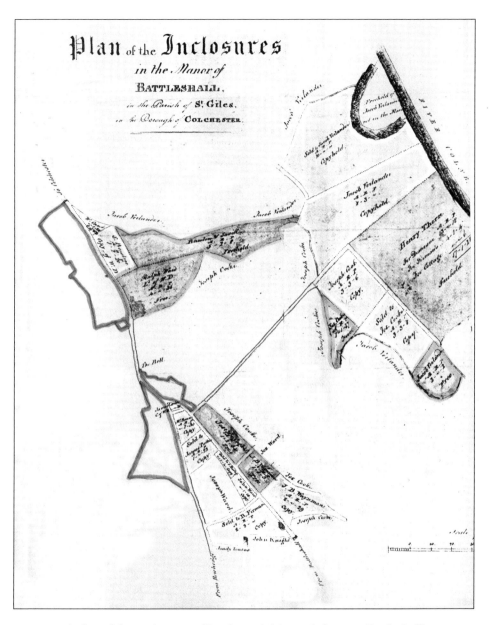

*A plan of the enclosures of Battleswick Manor (otherwise Battleshall)
as depicted in 1818. The three areas of enclosed land can be clearly
identified on Chapman and Andre's map.*

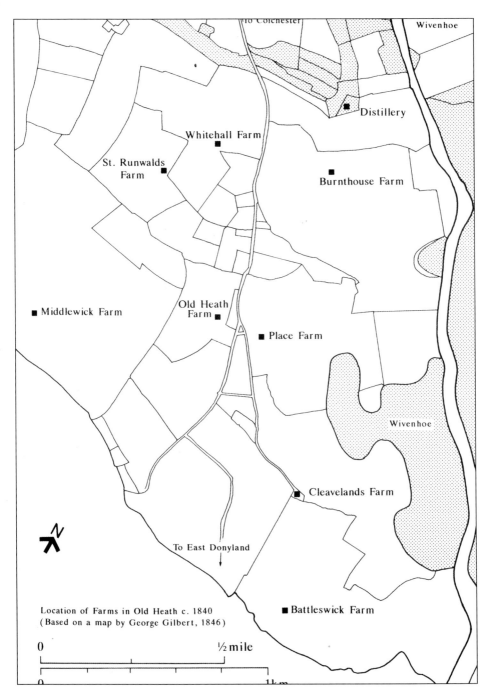

A map of Old Heath showing the principal landholdings in the 1840s.

12

Place Farm, Rowhedge Road in the 1980s. The farm buildings have since been demolished and replaced with a modern block of flats.

Known locally as 'The Lane' this narrow track running between Old Heath Road and Cavandish Avenue was formerly the entrance to Whitehall Farm.

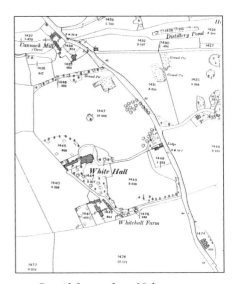

George Savill, former Mayor of Colchester (1835-36) and owner of the White Hall Estate. He was also part owner of the large malt distillery from which Distillery Pond takes its name.

Detail from a late 19th century Ordnance Survey map showing the White Hall Estate. Note the position of Cannock Mill and Distillery Pond in the top left and right corners.

The only known picture of White Hall. The land on which the building once stood has been given over to housing, although the name still survives in various street names.

Part of a sale catalogue relating to the disposal of the White Hall Estate following George Savill's death in 1847.

This early view of Bourne Pond and Mill dating from the 1850s has an interesting background. The wooded area to the right of the mill is part of the White Hall Estate, and White Hall itself can just be seen to the far right. To the left of the picture, between Bourne Mill and the cottage, can be seen Cannock Mill (on Old Heath Road), and if you look very carefully to the immediate left of Bourne Mill you can just make out the top of Old Heath Windmill rising above the trees. This mill stood on ground to the left of the old Whitehall Road and appears to have been demolished sometime in the early 1890s

COLCHESTER, ESSEX.

PARTICULARS
AND CONDITIONS OF SALE,
OF A VALUABLE FREEHOLD

ESTATE,
(LAND-TAX REDEEMED).

DISTINGUISHED AS

W·HITE HALL,

FOR MANY YEARS THE RESIDENCE OF THE LATE GEORGE SAVILL, Esquire,

VERY PLEASANTLY SITUATE, ONLY ONE-AND-A-HALF MILE FROM THE CENTRE OF THE ANCIENT BOROUGH TOWN OF COLCHESTER, AND BUT THREE-QUARTERS OF A MILE DISTANT FROM THE HYTHE TERMINUS OF THE STOUR VALLEY RAILWAY.

TOGETHER, WITH NEARLY

FIFTY-TWO ACRES

OF PASTURE AND ARABLE LAND, IN HIGH CULTIVATION;

Which will be Sold by Auction, by

MR. W. W. SIMPSON,

AT THE MART, LONDON,

On **TUESDAY**, the **21st day of September, 1847,**

AT TWELVE O'CLOCK.

The Property may be viewed by Cards, and Particulars may be obtained, of Messrs. PHILBRICK, Solicitors, Colchester; at the Mart; and of Mr. W. W. SIMPSON, 18, Bucklersbury, London.

ESSEX,

IN THE BOROUGH OF COLCHESTER.

Extensive & Valuable Freehold Property,

(INCLUDING A SMALL PORTION OF COPYHOLD),

CONNECTED WITH THE LATE MALT DISTILLERY.

Particulars and Conditions of Sale

OF AN EXCEEDINGLY

VALUABLE PROPERTY

(THE WHOLE EXONERATED FROM LAND TAX, AND THE GREATER PART FREEHOLD AND TITHE FREE),

COMPRISING

A capital Steam & Water Corn Mill,

A TOWER WINDMILL,

CAPACIOUS GRANARIES, COUNTING HOUSES,

STABLING & PREMISES;

TWO SUPERIOR RESIDENCES

WITH GARDENS, LAWNS, PLEASURE GROUNDS, AND

RICH MEADOW LAND ATTACHED;

A DWELLING HOUSE, occupied by the late Brewer,

PRODUCTIVE ORCHARD, GARDEN, AND MEADOW LAND ADJOINING,

Numerous PARCELS of ARABLE & MEADOW LAND,

Admirably adapted for Building on, and well calculated for Market Gardens and accommodation purposes;

ALSO,

VARIOUS PLOTS OF VALUABLE GROUND,

Abutting upon the navigable *River Colne*, suitable for the erection of Warehouses, Wharfs and Business Premises;

A VALUABLE MARSH,

CONTAINING NEARLY

EIGHTEEN ACRES.

AND A

Detached Arable Field, containing about Eight Acres,

WITH A

SUBSTANTIAL MESSUAGE AND SCHOOL ROOM ADJOINING;

THE ENTIRE PROPERTY COMPRISES NEARLY

ONE HUNDRED ACRES

of very superior Land, delightfully situated in the Parishes of St. BOTOLPH and St. GILES, and within about a mile of the Town of COLCHESTER, and presents a rare opportunity for advantageous Investment.

It will be Sold by Auction, by

Mr. W. W. SIMPSON,

AT THE CUPS HOTEL, COLCHESTER,

On TUESDAY, the 16th day of AUGUST, 1842,

AT TWELVE O'CLOCK, IN THIRTY-SEVEN LOTS.

An 1842 advertisement for the sale of the old distillery site and other land holdings in Old Heath. Note the inclusion of the tower windmill mentioned on the previous page.

16

Above: The original Bell Inn and cottages standing on what is now the greensward in front of the Congregational chapel - c.1930 Below: The same view in 2006.

The Bell Inn looking in the direction of Colchester in the early 1930s. The origin of the inn is lost in antiquity, but the building made headline news in 1884 when it was struck by the Great English Earthquake.

The Bell Inn looking towards Fingringhoe Road in the 1930s.

*These cottages opposite the Bell Inn have changed very little over the last 70 years.
In the early 1900s the cottage on the left was the local Post Office run by Mr Robert
Cranmer. Prior to this, during the 1880s and 1890s, the Post Office was located further
along the road on the site of the present garage (see P.O. sign on map page 23)*

The same viewpoint in 2006.

This interesting view shows both the old and the new Bell Inn standing side by side in 1938. Obviously the brewing company has resisted pulling down the old pub until the new one was up and running and drawing in customers

Old Heath Public Library and Reading Room. The library was opened in March 1892 by the Mayoress, Mrs Wilson Marriage, which was two years before the town's main library opened in West Stockwell Street. The building stood on land belonging to Mr James Malster who owned a timber yard and workshop in Fingringhoe Road.

Another before and after view of Old Heath Road
taken from near the junction with Rowhedge Road in 1930 (above)
and in 2006 (below)

Above: Many readers will recall the original Fish and Chip shop which stood in Fingringhoe Road - seen here in 1935.

Below: Its modern replacement continues to provide a welcome service to the community - 2006

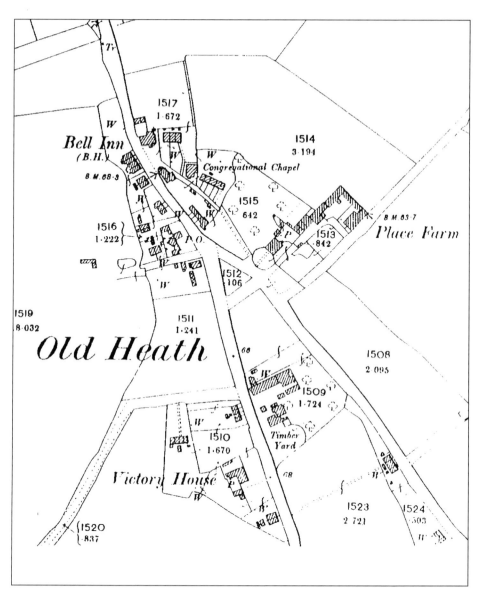

Detail from a late Victorian Ordnance Survey map of Old Heath. Note the site of the Post Office (P.O.) near the junction between Rowhedge and Fingringhoe Roads, and the profusion of wells (W) for water supply at the time.

Old Heath Road looking towards the Bell Inn in the 1930s. Note the lack of any made-up footpaths and the high hedge bordering the road.

A similar view to the above taken in recent times.

Rowhedge Road looking in the direction of Colchester - c 1990

*Fingringhoe Road looking in the direction of Colchester in the 1990s.
The Old Heath Library and Reading Room (see page 20) was located
somewhere near the bungalow on the right.*

This view of Old Heath Road from the early 1930s would be totally unrecognisable today were it not for the detached house standing on the right. The small brick-like structure standing on the left of the road was known locally as 'Jumbo' and contained a running spring of water for the use of passers by and local residents. The same view below, showing the playing field and entrance to Cottage drive on the left, was taken in 1994

The junction with Abbots Road and Old Heath Road as seen in the 1930s (above) and again in 2006 (below). Apart from one or two additional buildings the main difference between the two scenes is that the road is now full of traffic.
To the left of the older picture can be seen Heathfields House which for many years was the home of General Bruce Morland Skinner.

*In this scene from 1930 workmen can be seen clearing the ground for what was to become an access road to the Speedwell Road housing estate. Note that the excavation work is being carried out by hand and the spoil removed by horse and cart.
The work also appears to be quite labour intensive with at least nine workmen involved. Today the same operation would probably be carried out by a single operative using a mechanical digger.*

The modern-day view showing where 52 new houses were built between 1930 and 1933.

*Building work progressing on new housing in Cheveling Road
and Speedwell Road in 1935*

The same scene nearly 70 years on.

Another remarkable before and after scene showing how the village-like atmosphere of Old Heath has disappeared with the march of modern technology. One would expect that the generation of the 1930s received far more in the way of exercise than do their modern counterparts! (above 1935 - opposite page 2006)

Detail from a late Victorian Ordnance Survey map of Old Heath. Moy's Cottages, seen at the top of the map, complete with outside privies, are still standing, as is the Malthouse building which now forms part of Magnets Kitchen Showroom. Note also that Heathfields House was then known as The Limes.

Heathfields House as seen in the late 1980s. The house was originally the home of Richard Cuddon, a brewer from Abberton, who established a brewing and malting business here in the 1870s

Above: Abbots Road at its junction with Old Heath Road in 1931.
Below: The same view in 2006

*Old Heath Road looking in a north-westerly direction towards the junction
with D'arcy Road in the 1930s. The square-fronted building to the left of the picture
(where Magnet's now stands) was an off-licence, and at the end of the row of buildings
on the left can be seen the old timber-framed Co-op Hall.
Note also what a quiet looking road this appears to be.*

The same view as seen in 2006.

Old Heath Road looking south-east from a position between D'arcy Road and Abbots Road in c.1990. The row of six cottages on the left are known as Moy's Cottages, and were erected by Thomas Moy (coal merchant) sometime around the 1880s. Mr Moy owned what was then Burnt House Farm, which extended to about 100 acres. In later years it became known as Grange Farm (we still have Grange Farm Trailer Park) and covered an area which today encompasses most of the Whitehall Road Industrial Estate and the Sewage Treatment Works.

A snow-covered Old Heath Road looking in the direction of Colchester with the barrel-shaped roof of the Co-op Hall on the left - c.1990

*All that remains of a row of buildings that were demolished to make way
for the new access road to the Whitehall Industrial Estate. The monkey-puzzle tree
survived for several years until it was finally removed when the access
road was widened some years later.*

*The junction with Old Heath Road and Whitehall Road
as it appears today (2006).*

*With the exception of the Post Office building in the centre of this row of houses
on Old Heath Road from the 1930s, very little has changed in the intervening years.
A new footpath on the left, double-yellow lines, a pedestrian crossing island and
a number of small house extensions being among the notable exceptions.*

*Members of the Crick family outside their home at 210 Old Heath Road in 1920.
The young man leaning against the wall wearing a trilby hat is Frank Crick
who was born in the village in 1898. Not long after leaving Old Heath School
Frank emigrated to Saskatchewan in western Canada where for several years
he worked as a farm-hand and lumberjack. However, on his return to Canada shortly
after this picture was taken he joined the Royal Canadian Mounted Police.
Frank settled in Canada for the rest of his life and died in 1988.*

*The present occupant of 210 Old Heath Road is Maureen Davey seen here in 2006.
Maureen recalls that when Frank Crick made one of his rare visits home in the late
1960s, she and her late husband Robert were pleased to meet him and
show him round his old family home.*

Mountie Frank Crick, with his horse Sandy, on duty at Humboldt, Saskatchewan in 1925.

Old Heath Road looking towards Colchester near the junction with Cavendish Avenue

A 19th century view of Distillery Pond and Mill. The large house in the background is known as 'Maitlands', presumably so named after Robert Maitland Savill, who was one of the partners in the old distillery.

A fairly modern view of the pond showing the old laundry building before it was demolished to make way for housing - c.1990

Two contrasting views of Cannock Hill, looking towards Colchester, taken over 60 years apart. The top picture dates from the 1930s and captures the last of the great elm trees which once arched across the roadway creating a tunnel-like effect before their removal for house building.

Chapter Two
Schooldays

Old Heath Board School shortly after its construction in 1894.

The earliest confirmed school in Old Heath was that which opened on 14 March 1836 in a large room at the Bell Inn. The school was established by James Ashwell Tabor who at the time lived in Old Heath Cottage where Cottage Drive now stands.

It would seem that the hired room at the Bell Inn was just a temporary measure for in the following year Mr Tabor reports that he had taken possession of a new school room. His diary entry reads: "Took possession of the New School Room, 20 November 1837" This building survives as Savill Cottage (seen here) on the Old Heath Road opposite to the junction with Abbots Road. The single-storey extension seen at the rear of the building is all that remains of the old schoolroom which extended up to the main house. The head master's office was in the room to the right of the front entrance porch.

This is Jane Lever who was born in Old Heath in 1864 and who later became a pupil at the Savill Cottage schoolroom.

A sampler completed by Jane Lever when she was nine years old.

This view of St Barnabas' Chapel was taken shortly after the opening of the new Old Heath Board School which can be seen in the background. The chapel was opened in March 1875 and for 20 years doubled as a school during the week, and as a chapel for religious services at weekends.

Old Heath School - infant's class of 1898. Note the rocking horse on the left and the writing slates propped up on the fronts of the desks.

Old Heath School - c.1904. The head teacher, pictured with the bowler hat, was Archibald William Alderton who later transferred to East Ward School in 1908

Stanley Crick - born in Old Heath in 1887. Stanley first attended the old school/chapel building in Abbots Road before transferring, along with 70 other pupils, to the new Board School in November 1894.

COLCHESTER SCHOOL BOARD.

OLD HEATH SCHOOL.

Master - - - JNO. CHEESE.

Name *Stanley Crick,*

Subject *Writing.*

Date *March 1st 1897.*

H. G. ROGERS, STATIONER, COLCHESTER.

The cover label from young Stanley's writing exercise book dated March 1897.
Opposite page - an example of Stanley's transcription work. Not bad for a 10 year old!

Transcription

James V of Scotland, who reigned over that kingdom in the time of our English king Henry VIII had a custom of going about the country disguised as a private person, in order that he might hear complaints which might not otherwise reach his ears, and perhaps that he might enjoy amusements which he could not have partaken of in his avowed royal character. This is also said to have been a custom of James IV, his father, and several adventures are related which befell them on such occasions.

Boy pupils enjoying a breather from their labours in the school garden at Old Heath School in 1905. Gardening classes were very much a part of the school curriculum for boys in many Colchester schools. At some schools the boys were also allowed to keep a few chickens or pigeons to give them experience in animal husbandry.

Old Heath School - 1914. The teacher standing on the left is Walter Fuller, and standing at the rear of the class is the headmaster, Frank Bates. To the right of Mr Bates is Bert Crick, whose relations still live in Old Heath. Note the pinafore frocks worn by many of the girls, and the high starched collars and 'Norfolk' type jackets worn by some of the boys. Also note that the desks are all arranged in neat rows with the children seated in pairs and facing to the front of the class.

Leslie Crick (b.1906) who attended Old Heath School between 1911 and 1920.

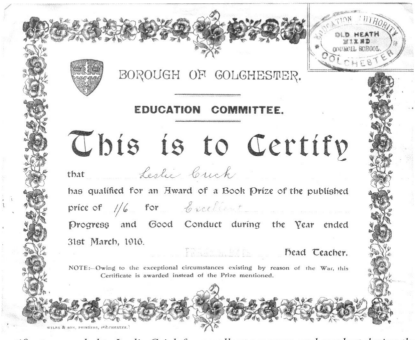

A certificate awarded to Leslie Crick for excellent progress and conduct during the year ended March 1916. Apparently, under normal circumstances Leslie would have received a book to the value of one shilling and sixpence (7½p), but owing to the problems associated with the continuing war had to make do with this certificate.

Old Heath School - c.1907. The boy on the extreme left of the group is Frank Crick (b.1898) who in the summer of 1909 was chosen along with nine other children from the school to appear in the great Colchester Pageant.

In this souvenir view of the Pageant some of the performers (some 3,500 local people took part) are seen taking part in the grand parade at the end of the performance

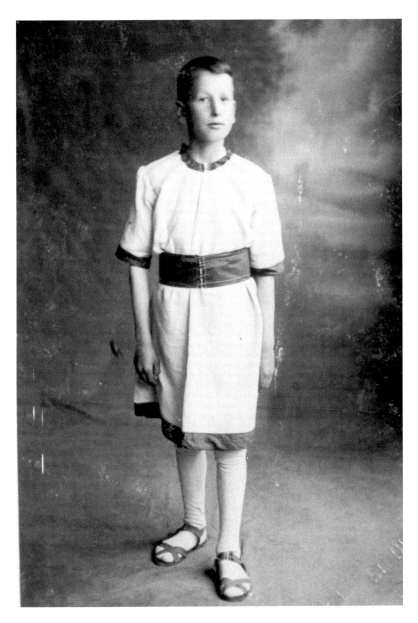

Frank Crick in his pageant costume. Frank played the part of a Roman Camilli (a young child employed in religious worship and ceremony).

These two views of Old Heath School choir were taken some 50 years apart. The top picture dates from around 1912 and includes the headmaster Mr Frank Bates. The lower picture is from 1961 and includes the headmaster Mr Frederick Richards. Note also the old World War II air raid shelter in the background.

Above: Old Heath School netball team in 1919 accompanied by Mr Bates (headmaster) and Miss Mason. Below: The school netball team from 1961 including (back row) Mr Richards (headmaster), Linda Partridge, Christine Crick, Miss Bareham (front row) Carol Kettleton, Jackie Mason, Jackie Mallett, Janet Halls and Jenny Wellham.

A view of Old Heath Road taken from outside the school in the 1930s and again in 2005. The bus in the older picture is probably that belonging to Mr Tom Fale of Rowhedge whose daily service to Colchester had developed from a horse-drawn carrier business in the early 1900s. The service survived until the 1960s before being taken over by the Eastern National Omnibus Company.

Old Heath School - 1947

Old Heath School - 1952

Old Heath School - 1955

Old Heath School - 1959

Old Heath School football team in 1960

Old Heath School football team in 1976. The teacher is Mr Beale

Pupils hard at work in their classroom in about 1980.
The teacher is Mr Brian Bakowski.

Old Heath School - a slightly more informal grouping from about 1982.

Old Heath School reunion - February 2002.
The event was held in the school hall with nearly
a hundred former pupils in attendance.

Daniel Chapman (aged 12) and his grandfather, former pupil Steve Bailey, were both in attendance at the reunion.

Pleased to meet you - the oldest and youngest pupils attending the event were Ryan Everitt (aged 9) and Edna Mills (aged 83).

Chapter Three
Church and Chapel

St Barnabas' school/chapel which opened on 23 March 1875. The building, which cost £564 to erect and had room for 130 worshipers, was used as a school during the week and as a chapel at weekends

St Barnabas' Church pictured sometime in the early 1930s. This was a chapel of ease to St Giles' in Colchester until it attained parochial status in 1950.

The same view of Abbots Road showing the modern church in 2006.

St Barnabas' Church, Abbots Road - c.1940. Note the presence of the new church hall, erected in 1938, and the absence of the small bell tower.

The interior of St Barnabas' Church in 1925.

This picture shows the interior of St Barnabas' Church in 1927 following some substantial restoration work. The chancel windows have disappeared and the internal brickwork covered up. A new oak altar and reredos, together with matching panelling have also been introduced to the chancel.

A close up view of the renovated chancel showing the addition of a new oak chancel screen and rood - c.1928.

The 1927 altar and reredos were retained from the old church when it was demolished in the 1950s and re-installed in the present Lady Chapel.

The present St Barnabas' Church which was built in 1955. Like its predecessor, this was also intended as a dual purpose building (for both religious and secular use) but it has only ever been used as a church.

Fr Richard Tillbrook standing in the nave of the present church in 2006. The pulpit (left corner) and pews were taken from St Nicholas' Church in Colchester High Street when it was pulled down in 1955. The Lady Chapel, where the oak panelling from the old church was installed, can be seen in the far right corner.

St Barnabas' Church choir - c.1925. Pictured on the left in the front row is the Rev. C. Haig (curate of St Giles') and seated behind the young boy on the ground is the Rev. John Evans (nicknamed Tubby Evans), rector of St Giles' and St Barnabas'. The young lad on the extreme right of the picture is Jack Denney who was later to lose his life in the Second World War. His elder brother, Alfred Denney, was killed in the First World War and his name is recorded on brass plaque in the church.

St Barnabas' Church choir in the late 1940s. The vicar seated in the front row is the Rev. George Cooper.

St Barnabas' choir - 2006.

Choir boy David Laitt pictured in 1958

This picture was taken to mark a Confirmation ceremony held in St Barnabas' Church in June 1983. The vicar on the left is Fr Brian Lewis and in background is John Trillo, Bishop of Chelmsford.

Old Heath Congregational Church in 2006. The original chapel was erected in 1869 as an outreach mission station of Lion Walk, although there had been a congregational presence in Old Heath since 1843 (possibly meeting in the Savill Cottage schoolroom, see p.43). The chapel was enlarged in 1888 and again in 1898. In the 1980s when Lion Walk became a United Reformed church, Old Heath became independent and retained its congregational status

An interior view of Old Heath Congregational Chapel taken at the time of the Harvest Festival (date unknown)

Chapter Four
Occupations and Trade

Delivery drivers and staff at Associated Biscuit Manufacturers depot on Old Heath Road line up for a group photograph in 1934. The manager of the depot was Fred Wheeler, seen here fourth from the right. His son, Ron Wheeler, who provided this photograph, also worked as a manager for the company. The warehouse building, which was originally constructed as a malthouse in the 1870s, still survives as part of Magnet's Kitchen Showroom.

James Brown's grocery shop on Fingringhoe Road in the 1930s. The ladies pictured are James's wife Priscilla (left) and his daughter Clara

Sign of the times! James Brown's former premises pictured in 2006.

Another member of the Crick family - this time George Crick (born 1892), seen standing in the door-way of his small boot and shoe repair business in Old Heath Road. George had become disabled through injuries received during the First World War and like many casualties of the conflict received occupational re-training in one of Lord Robert's Workshops. However, despite the success of his little enterprise he finally succumbed to his injuries and died in 1926.

Here is George (second from right) during his training in London with other casualties of the war being taught the boot and shoe repair trade.

One of the town's early motorists was McGregor Mason, proprietor of Old Heath Motorcycle and Cycle Store. This photograph was taken outside the original shop in Fingringhoe Road and shows Mr Mason with his children and family car. In earlier years this was the local post office, general store and butchers.

*Mason's garage as seen in the 1930s
and its modern equivalent in 2006.*

Hythe Maltings pictured sometime in the early 1900s. The maltings were erected in the 1850s and included four cottages for the malt workers.

It is not clear what these workmen are doing on the riverbed just below the Hythe maltings (date unknown)

Workers employed at Dobson's brickfields, Cleavelands Farm, Old Heath, in 1901. The bricks laid out on the left-hand barrow have yet to be fired, while those on the right have been removed from the kilns at the rear.

Another view of the brickfields showing brick-maker Alf Crick (right) and his son Sidney. Sidney's job was to load the newly made bricks onto a flat barrow called a hack (designed to carry 26 bricks) before transporting them to the open-air drying sheds

Chapter Five
Wartime

Pupils at Old Heath School pictured with Red Cross workers some time around the start of the First World War.

Local Civil Defence Volunteers practising their first aid and fire prevention skills in the school playground.

The full contingent of the Old Heath Civil Defence Volunteers in the school playground. Notice the air vent leading from the air raid shelter in the background.

Old Heath Laundry as it appeared in 1930. On 3 October 1940, the building was shattered when it received a direct hit from an enemy bomber. Fortunately most of the staff had left the building for their mid-day break, but three girls who were sitting in the mess room eating their lunch when the bomb dropped were killed instantly.

The aftermath of the bombing raid showing the extent of the devastation. In nearby Scarletts Road a pair of houses were also hit in the same raid resulting in the death of a mother and her five year old son.

Local youngsters line up for an end of war fancy dress parade in Canwick Grove - 1945

Canwick Grove in 2006.

The VE Day party atmosphere continued on Middlewick (on the site of the present Mountbatten housing estate) where local residents posed for this group photograph

This street party was laid on for the residents of both Foresight Road and Speedwell Road in May 1945.

Chapter Six
Events and Leisure

In this picture of the Old Heath Bell workmen can be seen making repairs to part of the roof following damage caused by the Great Earthquake of 1884.

A 1930s view of Old Heath Road looking towards Colchester near the present junction with D'arcy Road. The low timber building in the centre of the picture was erected in the early 1920s as a social club for local residents. Also just beyond the small lorry about to disappear from view can be seen George Crick's small boot and shoe repair building standing by the roadside (see p.71).

Members of Old Heath Sports and Social Club standing outside their clubhouse in Old Heath Road, c.1922. Pictured from the left are: Les Crick, Reg Pettican, Eddie Allen (rear), Bob Allen (front), Eddie Amos and Mr Brindley. The building itself was an old army hut which had been adapted and erected by the club members themselves. Prior to this the group had met in a room at the old brewery (now Magnets) which was owned by Major General Skinner from Heathfields House.

In the early hours of Friday, 1 December 1950 the Old Heath clubhouse, which by this time was owned by the Co-op, was badly damaged by fire. It was reported at the time that had it not been for a favourable wind fanning the flames away from the building, the clubhouse would have been totally destroyed.

The Old Heath Co-operative Hall building shortly before its demolition in 2000.

The Co-op Hall in the 1990s - a place for socialising and for entertainment.

Members of the Old Heath Bell Quoits team in 1913. The man seated on the left is William Motts, the landlord, and the lady on the right is his wife.

The Old Heath Bell Quoits team of 1923. The man seated second from the left in the front row is wearing a silver war badge on his right lapel, indicating that he may have been wounded during the First World War. The badge was issued to everyone who had been forced to retire from active service through either sickness or injury and was intended to allay any accusations of cowardice for being out of uniform.

Old Heath Boys Brigade pictured about 1947. The picture was taken in the old rectory garden, next to the church hall, in Abbots Road. The group paraded every Sunday with a band and alternated, on a weekly basis, between St Barnabas' Church and the Congregational Chapel. Eventually, a division occurred between both denominations and the group was finally disbanded.

This picture taken in Old Heath appears to be some kind of church social gathering - possibly in connection with St Barnabas'. Judging by the group's clothing, and the women's hairstyles, the picture would seem to pre-date the First World War.

St Barnabas' Summer Fayre and Flower Show in July 1944. The picture was taken in the school playground and includes the Mayor, Councillor Maurice Pye and the Rev. B. Pemberton

Members of Old Heath Rabbit Club pictured in the school playground in 1949. The group was formed at the end of the war in 1945.

*Members of Old Heath Townswomen's Guild at the time
of their 25th anniversary in 1977.*

These local children are being treated to a special tea party in Cavendish Avenue to celebrate the Coronation of Queen Elizabeth in June 1953.

Part of the Coronation celebrations included a children's fancy dress parade as can be seen from these two photographs.

Old Heath Community Fun Day, September 2005. One lucky visitor at the tombola stall appears to have hit the jackpot!

This picture was taken in the vicarage garden to celebrate the success of the local street warden initiative. Those gathered include members of the street warden team, the Mayor of Colchester, councillor Terry Sutton, local councillors Mary Blandon and Justin Knight and Liberal Democrat MP for Colchester Bob Russell.

*Members of the 21st Colchester Scout Troop who held their meetings at St Barnabas'
Church Hall, Old Heath. The picture was taken at Hockley at the time of the Essex
Scout Jamboree in 1960.*

This picture shows Old Heath cub Derek Keeble demonstrating his camping skills -c.1980.
Photograph by kind permission of the Evening Gazette

The 9th Colchester Old Heath cub pack pictured in the old prison cells at the Town Hall in 1978. The cub scout leader seen on the right is Olwyn Powell

*These cubs from Old Heath are celebrating winning
the Eastern District Cubs Sports event in June 1971*

*This picture shows the 2nd Old Heath Brownies at their Christmas Party in 1955.
Standing behind the table are (from the left) Penny Jackson (pack leader),
Brenda Blowers (pack leader) Hilda Pearce (Tawny Owl), Joan Brown (Brown Owl)
and Yvonne Pearce (pack leader)*

The 2nd Old Heath Brownie pack pictured in the school playground in 1959.

These members of the 2nd Old Heath Brownies pictured in 1953 are (from the left)
Gillian Marshall, Rosemary Clark, Angela Tyler and Jeannette Munson

The wedding of 'Tawny Owl' Sue Hall to Roy Cansdale in 1984.

The 2nd Old Heath Girl Guides pictured in the school hall in 1957.